Sound

First published 2020
Foxton Books
London, UK

Copyright © Foxton Books, 2020

ISBN: 978-1-83925-008-8

Written by Nichola Tyrrell
Designed by Maryke Goldie
Logo design: Stewart Wright (2Wright Design)
Cover design: Ed White
Education consultant: Frances Barlow

About Foxton Primary Science:

The Foxton Primary Science series supports Key Stage 1, Lower Key Stage 2
and Upper Key Stage 2 Science.

This title supports the Sound section of **Lower Key Stage 2** Science through a variety
of features and **STEAM**-inspired tasks that cover all curriculum requirements.

Colourful, engaging content blends information with prompts
for further discussion and investigation.

Keywords, creative activities and quizzes reinforce comprehension,
along with challenging words (in bold) explained in the glossary.

Contents

Surrounded by sound 4

Sound waves 6

What is volume? 8

What is pitch? 10

Activity: Water glass pitch 12

How sound travels 14

Activity: Travelling whispers 16

Musical instruments 18

Activity: Make a harmonica 20

How ears work 22

Let's experiment: Muffling sound 24

Comprehension check 28

Vocabulary check 29

Glossary 30

Index and answers 32

Surrounded by sound

The world is filled with sounds. They can be loud or quiet, like the beep of a car or the pitter-patter of rain. Sounds can be long or short, like a baby crying or a single tap on a table.

Sounds can tell you what something is and where it is.

Keywords sound vibration

We recognise the sound of an audience clapping.

squeezing

clapping

Sounds happen when an object moves or vibrates. We make an object vibrate in different ways, like banging, tearing and squeezing.

The vibrations are invisible. They travel through the air and into your ear.

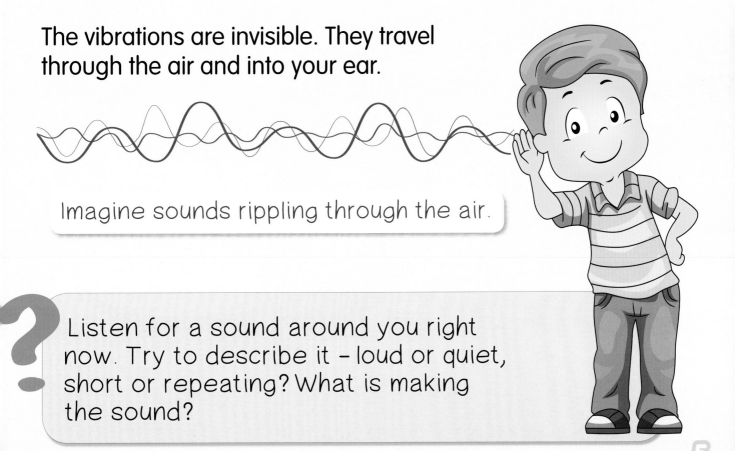

Imagine sounds rippling through the air.

? Listen for a sound around you right now. Try to describe it – loud or quiet, short or repeating? What is making the sound?

Sound waves

A **vibration** is the fast movement of something from side to side or back and forth. Stretch a rubber band with your hands. Ask a friend to pluck it with a finger. Notice how the band moves. That is vibration.

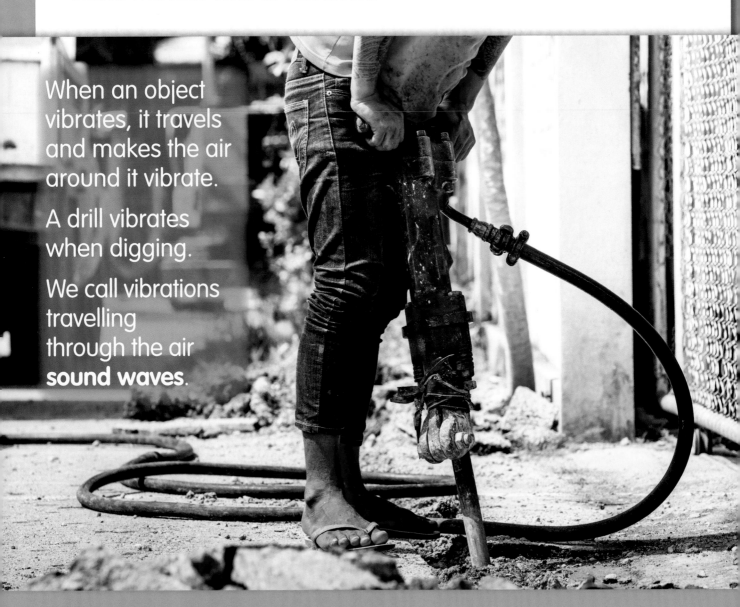

When an object vibrates, it travels and makes the air around it vibrate.

A drill vibrates when digging.

We call vibrations travelling through the air **sound waves**.

Keywords eardrum   sound wave

We can't see sound waves, but they move outward from their **source**, in all directions, and then fade.

Sound waves travel outward, like ripples in a puddle.

When speaking or singing, vocal cords in the throat make the air vibrate. When the travelling vibrations (sound waves) hit the eardrum, we hear them as sounds.

Sound travels fast! Sound waves travel from their source at 343 metres per second. That is almost the length of four football fields put together!

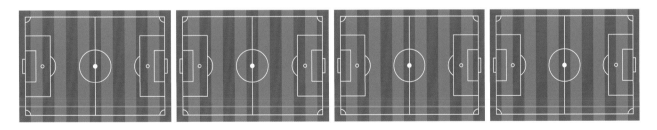

Put your hand on your throat and hum. What can you feel?

What is volume?

Volume is the loudness of a sound. We refer to high and low volume for loud and quiet. We turn volume up and down to increase and decrease it.

Strength of the vibration **determines** if a sound is loud or quiet.

Keywords   decrease   increase   volume

We can increase or decrease the volume of a musical instrument by playing it in different ways. The softer you blow into a recorder, the quieter the sound.

If the source of the sound moves, the volume changes. The closer a moving siren becomes, the louder the sound.

Make a kazoo by folding tissue paper over the teeth of a comb. Press your lips against the side of the comb and hum through it. Experiment with making the sound louder or quieter.

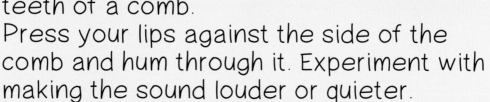

What is pitch?

The pitch of a sound is how high or low the sound is. A high sound has a high pitch and a low sound has a low pitch.

Blowing a whistle makes a high pitch sound.

Thunder has a low pitch.

lightning

The faster an object vibrates, the higher the pitch of the sound. The slower the vibration, the lower the sound.

What is it that makes these vibrations, or sound waves, different?

There are some sound waves that only animals can hear. Dogs can hear high-pitched sounds that humans can't.

Water glass pitch

Try this simple activity with drinking glasses to hear different levels of pitch and learn how different amounts of material can affect sound.

You will need:

- 4 tall drinking glasses
- water
- food colouring
- spoon

spoon

water glass

food colouring

1. Place the glasses side by side in a row, but not touching each other.

2. Fill the first glass with water until it's nearly full.

3. Fill the other glasses with different amounts of water, so each contains less than the glass before it.

4. Add a drop of food colouring to each glass so it's easy to see the different amounts.

5. Gently tap the side of each glass with a spoon.

- Which glass makes the highest sound?
- Which makes the lowest?
- Do glasses vibrate slower when they contain less water?

Different water levels will make different sounds when you tap the glass. Tapping the glass vibrates the water, which vibrates the air into sound waves.

Try to make up a tune with your musical glasses!

How sound travels

Sound must travel through a material. We know sound travels through air, which is a gas. It can also travel through solids and liquids. How does the type of material affect a sound?

If the music playing in a closed car is loud enough, we can hear it outside of the car. The sound waves are travelling through metal, glass and plastic.

Keywords gas liquid solid

In the water glass activity on page 12, the glass with the most water had the lowest sound, or pitch. This is because the vibrations were slower as they had more water to travel through than the other glasses.

When sound waves hit some hard surfaces, the waves bounce back and can be heard a second time. This is an echo.

gymnasium

We can make an echo from a distance in places with hard walls or with hard surfaces all around. An empty school gymnasium is likely to produce an echo.

Shouting in a canyon or a valley between mountains is likely to produce an echo.

Travelling whispers

Imitate the very first telephone to feel sound waves travelling.

You will need:
- 2 metres of string or yarn/wool
- 1 paper cup
- 1 paper clip
- pencil
- a partner making the same thing

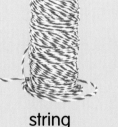

string

paper cup

paper clip

Experiment with the cup to find out what you can hear and feel when speaking into it.

1. Tie a knot at one end of the string to form a loop.

2. Open the paper clip and slide on the loop of string.

3. Take the two ends and twist them apart.

4. Poke a hole through the bottom of the cup with your pencil.

5. Push the paper clip through the hole; this will stop the string from coming out.

6. Tie the loose end of your string to the loose end of your partner's string.

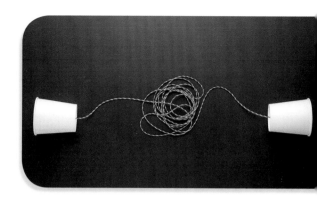

Your telephone is complete. Decide who will be the 'ear' first and who will be the 'voice'.

7. Spread out your string so it is straight. The 'voice' person whispers a number into their cup.

The 'ear' person then holds up the number of fingers to show what they heard!

Experiment with different materials to see if it makes a difference. Swap your string for ribbon, perhaps.

Musical instruments

Musical instruments make sound by vibrating in different ways. Music is a mixture of sounds that are **arranged** to make a tune.

Guitars make sound when their strings vibrate. What other stringed instruments can you think of?

Keywords instrument music notes

Most instruments are **tuned** to make different sounds we call notes. The notes are played in a particular order to play a song or tune.

A piano has different keys that play high pitch notes and low pitch notes.

Big instruments often have a low pitch and loud volume.

A drum produces sound when it's banged, making its skin vibrate up and down.

We blow into a wind instrument to make the air inside vibrate.

Make a harmonica

Explore how to change volume and pitch with a home-made harmonica.

You will need:
- 2 craft sticks
- 1 large rubber band
- 1 smaller rubber band
- 1 drinking straw
- scissors

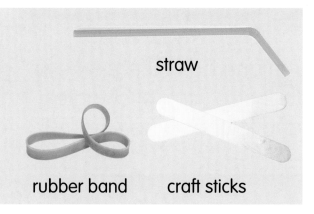

straw

rubber band   craft sticks

1. Decorate your sticks with paint or coloured pens.

2. Stretch the large rubber band lengthwise over one of the sticks.

3. Cut two pieces of straw, each measuring 3 centimetres.

4. Place one piece of straw under the rubber band, about 3 centimetres in from one end of the stick.

5. Place the other piece of straw on top of the rubber band, about 3 centimetres in from the other end of the stick.

6. Put the second stick on top of the first stick.

7. Wrap the smaller rubber bands around each end of the sticks, tying them together. You should see space between the sticks. If not, the bands are too tight.

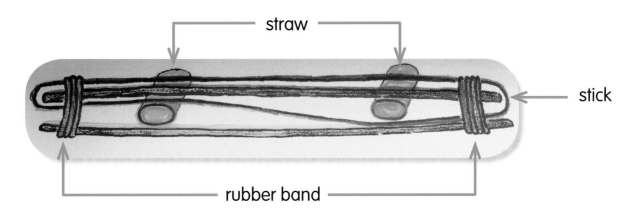

straw

stick

rubber band

Your harmonica is now ready to play!

Blow through the sticks (avoiding the straws). Blow hard and blow softly. Is there a difference in the sound?

Move the straws closer together and blow.
Does that make a difference?

The science part: when you blow into the harmonica, you are making the big rubber band vibrate, which makes the sound. When you move the straws closer together, you reduce the amount of the band that can vibrate. This makes the pitch higher.

How ears work

When a sound wave reaches the ear, it takes a journey inside and eventually sends a message to the brain that there is a sound happening.

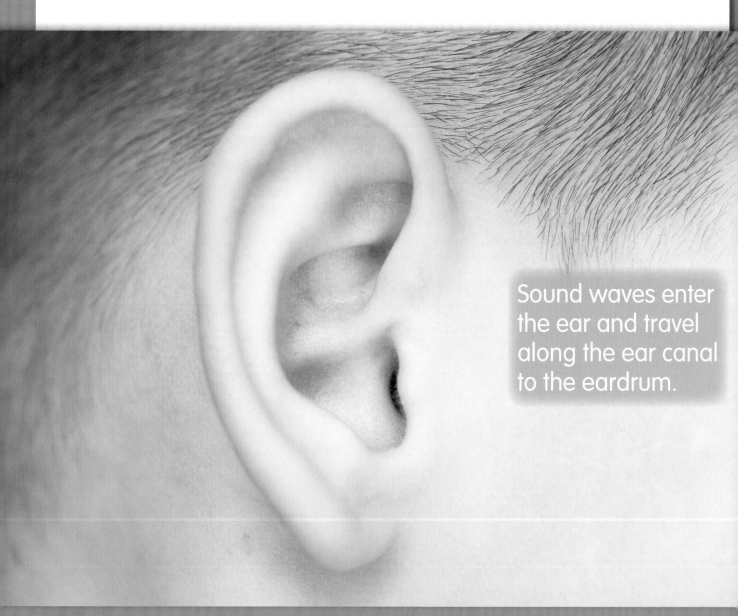

Sound waves enter the ear and travel along the ear canal to the eardrum.

Keywords brain ear canal

1. The eardrum is a thin flap of skin that is stretched tight like a drum. Sound waves make it vibrate.

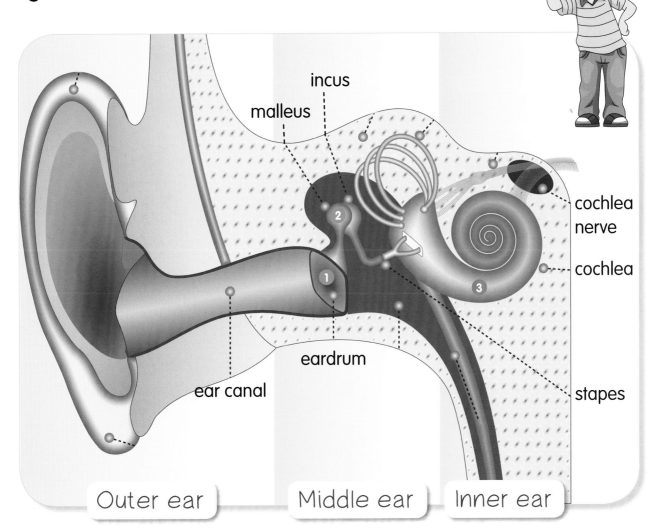

incus

malleus

cochlea nerve

cochlea

eardrum

ear canal

stapes

Outer ear   Middle ear   Inner ear

2. On the other side of the eardrum are the body's smallest bones: the malleus, incus and stapes. These tiny bones vibrate when sound waves enter the middle ear.

3. The sound waves carry on further to the inner ear. Here, a part called the cochlea (shaped like a French horn) turns the sound waves into an electrical signal.

The signal travels along a nerve to the brain, which tells us the signal is a sound.

Materials for muffling

We know sound can travel through materials, including all sorts of solids. But some materials can muffle, or quieten, a sound so well we can barely hear it. Which materials are good for muffling sound?

You will need:

- two maracas or bells
- materials such as: a tea towel, newspaper, thick card, tin foil, wool scarf, bubble wrap

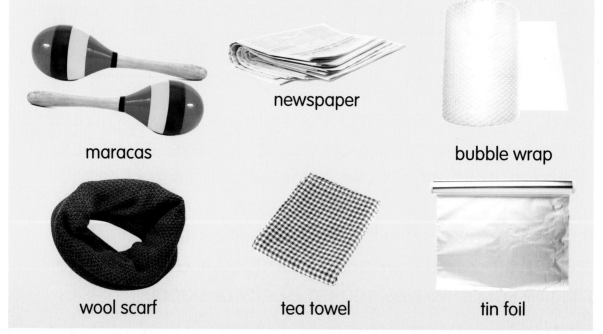

maracas

newspaper

bubble wrap

wool scarf

tea towel

tin foil

To ensure your test is fair:

Wrap two layers of each material around the maracas, leaving no openings.

Your method:

Wrap the maracas in different materials to be tested and shake them.

Compare the volume between the two. Then compare the loudest of the two against the next material, and then the next one, until all materials have been tested.

Record your observations and results. Photocopy or copy-draw this chart.

Observations and results for muffling the sound of a shaking maraca

Name: _____

Date: _____

Material	How did the maraca sound?	How well did it muffle sound compared to other materials?

Which material was best at muffling the sound of the maraca?

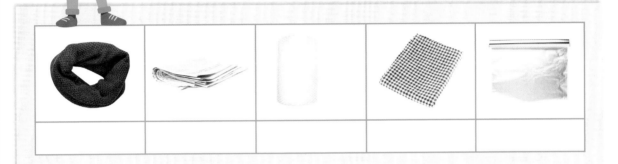

Now write up a report describing your experiment and the results.

Include these points:
- what you were trying to find out
- which materials were tested
- how you tested the materials
- the results of your experiment

Find and print out online pictures of each material used, and a maraca, and include these in your report.

Comprehension check

1. What do we call vibrations that are travelling through the air?

2. Is the sound of a whistle blowing a high pitch sound or a low pitch?

3. Can sound travel through liquids?

4. Can sound travel through solids?

5. You have a full glass of water and a glass that's nearly empty. If you tap each glass, which one will make the lower pitch sound?

6. Name a place that is likely to give an echo.

7. What do we call a mixture of sounds that are arranged to make a tune?

8. In the ear, what is the thin flap of skin that vibrates when sound waves enter the ear canal?

9. Can dogs hear high-pitched or low-pitched sounds that humans can't hear?

10. Which way do sound waves travel from their source: straight ahead or all around?

Turn to page 32 to mark your answers.

Vocabulary check

1. Sounds happen when an object moves or v _ _ _ _ _ _ _ .

2. The p _ _ _ _ of a sound is how high or low the sound is.

3. V _ _ _ _ _ is the loudness of a sound.

4. When sound waves hit some hard surfaces, the waves bounce back and can be heard a second time. This is an e _ _ _ .

5. Most i _ _ _ _ _ _ _ _ _ _ are tuned to make different sounds we call notes.

6. In the inner ear, the cochlea turns sound waves into an e _ _ _ _ _ _ _ _ _ signal.

7. Materials can m _ _ _ _ _ , or quieten, a sound so well we can barely hear it.

8. When speaking or singing, v _ _ _ _ c _ _ _ _ in the throat make the air vibrate.

9. Sound must travel through a m _ _ _ _ _ _ _ .

10. The f _ _ _ _ _ an object vibrates, the higher the pitch of the sound.

Turn to page 32 to mark your answers.

Sound check

Test yourself and your friends with a sound check challenge! Each participant should record a selection of different sounds and challenge partners to recognise them.

SOUND CHECK!

Choose a variety of sounds such as:

a flushing toilet

running water

whistling

a kettle boiling

clicking fingers

Glossary

Definitions relate to the context of word usage in this book.

arrange – to put things in a certain order

echo – when sound waves hit a hard surface and bounce back, to be heard a second time

gas – a form of matter that is neither liquid nor solid

note – a single musical tone

pitch – the description of how high or low a sound is

sound wave – vibrations travelling through the air

source – the start or cause of something

tune – musical notes played in a particular order

vibration – the fast movement of something from side to side or back and forth

vocal cords – folds in the windpipe (a tube between the throat and lungs) that produce the sound of the voice; the cords vibrate air to make sounds

volume – the level of loudness of a sound

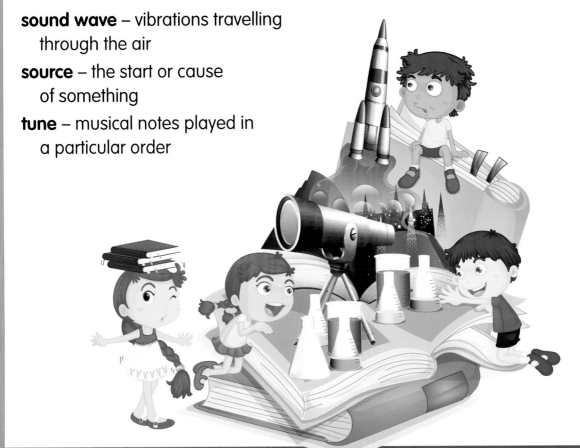

Index

ears   22–23

echo   15

harmonica-making   20–21

instruments   18, 19

kazoo-making   9

lightning   11

music   18–19

pitch   10–11, 12, 13, 20, 21

sound waves   6–7, 11, 15, 23

thunder   11

vibration   5, 8, 11, 15, 18, 19

volume   8, 9, 19

Quiz answers

Comprehension check, page 28

1. sound waves 2. high pitch

3. yes 4. yes 5. the full glass

6. a big empty room, a canyon or a valley

7. music 8. eardrum

9. high pitched 10. all around

Vocabulary check, page 29

1. vibrates 2. pitch 3. volume

4. echo 5. instruments

6. electrical 7. muffle 8. vocal cords

9. material 10. faster

Photo credits

Shutterstock.com: Cover: Artem Furman; pp 1–2: GraphicsRF, Anastacia - azzzya; pp 4–5: Khwanchai_s, Anneka, Lorelyn Medina, Idutko, Liubou Yasiukovich; pp 6–7: IRIT3530, Laurentiu Timplaru, narikan, SpeedKingz; pp 8–9: Photographee.eu, Fertas, Christin Lola, autsawin uttisin, Jakkarin chuenaka, Lorelyn Medina; pp 10–11: Martin Novak, John D Sirlin, Robert Neumann, Liubou Yasiukovich, yusufdemirci; pp 12–13: Lorelyn Medina, pirtuss, Luis Molinero, Elizabeth A.Cummings, Eva BB, Lorelyn Medina; pp 14–15: BEAUTY STUDIO, Luis Molinero, ikumaru, Sandra Foyt; pp 16–17: Warut Chinsai, ONYXprj, Dan Kosmayer, Evgenyrychko, Piyawat Nandeenopparit (x 2), unge255_photostock, Dualororua, Iconic Bestiary; pp 18–19: Fabio Principe, Vikulin, TEEREXZ, Dizfoto, Maja Marjanovic; pp 20–21: Yuriy Golub, Stephen Orsillo, New Africa, Feng Yu, Lec Neo, GraphicsRF (x 2), Lorelyn Medina; pp 22–23: donikz, Fouad A. Saad, Lorelyn Medina; pp 24–25: Lorelyn Medina, photo one, exopixel, NisanatStudio, Amelia Fox, artenot, Olya Detry, Iconic Bestiary, Diamond_Images; pp 26–27: Lorelyn Medina, Teguh Mujiono, Dualororua, schwarzhana, vitaliy_73, goir, mdbildes, NotionPic, NisanatStudio, Helen Stebakov, exopixel; pp 28–29: yusufdemirci; pp 30–32: Yurchenko Yulia, GraphicsRF, Teguh Mujiono

Pixabay.com: p 7: 12019; p 30: Svyatoslav, Maaark, Pezibear, Josch13, maxknoxvill